The Houses of
the Oireachtas

John McGowan Smyth

INSTITUTE OF PUBLIC ADMINISTRATION

Dublin

Published by
Institute of Public Administration
59 Lansdowne Road
Dublin 4 Ireland

First edition 1961
Second edition 1964
Third edition 1973
Fourth edition 1979

*Set in 11/12 Baskerville by Joe Healy Typesetting, and printed by
Cahill Printers Limited, Dublin.*

Contents

Preface

Various changes have been made in the procedures of the Houses since the publication of the third edition of this book in 1973. Consequential revisions of the text have kindly been undertaken in respect of the Dáil by Mr. Aidan Doyle, Clerk-Assistant of the Dáil and in respect of the Seanad by Mr. John R. Tobin, Clerk of the Seanad. I am extremely indebted to these former colleagues of mine. Without their help this edition would not have been possible.

Introduction

The 1937 Constitution (Article 15.1) of the Republic of Ireland states that the Oireachtas (National Parliament) shall consist of the President and two Houses: a House of Representatives to be called Dáil Éireann and a Senate to be called Seanad Éireann.

This book outlines the functions and powers of the two Houses and the procedures adopted by them in the discharge of their responsibilities. Such functions, powers and procedures derive first from the Constitution and secondly from law and the rules and standing orders made by the Houses pursuant to the provisions of the Constitution.

In the course of the book, references are made to the constitutional position, procedures and practices of other countries, not to underline any particular differences but to indicate that Ireland's system is one only of a number of systems in use in democratic countries.

While Ireland's parliamentary procedure might appear to be very complicated to the uninitiated, it must be remembered that it is carefully designed to ensure that the members have adequate opportunity to discuss proposals both in a general and in a detailed way and at the same time that business is transacted with reasonable expedition. The procedure is modelled on the British system and many of its detailed forms are explicable only by reference to British tradition and practice. Constitutional differences are not to any great extent reflected in procedure, which is determined more by the relationship between the legislature and the executive; this is generally the same in both countries.

Differences in procedure arise mainly from practical considerations: the congestion of business in the House of

Commons necessitates elaborate time-tables, the committal of most bills to standing committees, the limitation of debates on the estimates to a certain number of supply days and the selection of amendments by the Speaker, none of which is necessary in Ireland nor, indeed, in many other countries which have adopted the British model.

Ireland, in common with many other countries, has adapted to its own needs a system which has worked successfully for a considerable number of years, retaining what proved to be useful and rejecting the unnecessary and superfluous such as certain traditional British rituals. The forms are not sacrosanct, and adequate powers are available for adaptation in the light of changing circumstances.

1 Composition of the Houses

Dáil Éireann

The Constitution (Article 16.2) provides that the Dáil shall be composed of members who represent constituencies determined by law, and that, while the number of members shall from time to time be fixed by law, the total number shall not be fixed at less than one member for each thirty thousand of the population nor at more than one member for each twenty thousand of the population.

The constituencies are revised by the Oireachtas, pursuant to the provisions of the same article, at least once every twelve years, and notice is taken of changes in the distribution of the population since the previous revision. At present there are one hundred and forty-eight members and forty-two constituencies (based on the 1971 census figure of 2,978,248 population). The Constitution (Article 16.2.6°) further provides that no law shall be enacted whereby the number of members to be returned for any constituency shall be less than three.

The following table updates the information in *Representative Government in Ireland* by J. L. McCracken (Oxford University Press, London, 1958).

Table 1: Number of members and constituencies

Electoral Act	Number of constituencies	Constituencies returning						Total number of members
		9	8	7	5	4	3	
1923	30*	1	3	5	9	4	8	153
1935	34	–	–	3	8	8	15	138
1947	40	–	–	–	9	9	22	147
1961	38	–	–	–	9	12	17	144
1969	42	–	–	–	2	14	26	144
1974	42	–	–	–	6	10	26	148

*Includes the two university constituencies, each of which returned three members.

3

Seanad Éireann

The Seanad, pursuant to Article 18 of the Constitution, is composed of sixty members of whom:
1. eleven are nominated directly to the House by the Taoiseach (Head of the Government or Prime Minister)
2. three are elected by the National University of Ireland
3. three are elected by the University of Dublin
4. forty-three are elected from five panels of candidates containing respectively the names of persons having knowledge and practical experience of certain interests and services.
The Seventh Amendment of the Constitution (Election of Members of Seanad Éireann by Institutions of Higher Education) Bill 1979, which was approved by the people by a referendum held on 5 July 1979, provides for the election by universities and other institutions of higher education specified by law of such number of members of Seanad Éireann, not exceeding six, as may be specified by law. Those so elected would be in substitution for an equal number of the members elected at present by the National University of Ireland and the University of Dublin. No law as referred to has yet been enacted. Pursuant to section 43 of the Seanad Electoral (Panel Members) Act, 1947, the panels are each divided into sub-panels, one of which (Oireachtas sub-panel) contains the name of each candidate nominated by not less than four members of the Houses of the Oireachtas; the second (Nominating Bodies sub-panel) contains the names of those candidates nominated by bodies on the register of nominating bodies.

At present the number of members elected from each panel is divided as follows (section 52 of the Seanad Electoral (Panel Members) Act, 1947):
1. five members from the cultural and educational panel (representing the national language and culture, literature, art, education, law and medicine—including surgery, dentistry, veterinary medicine and pharmaceutical chemistry), of whom two at least are elected from each sub-panel;
2. eleven members from the agricultural panel (representing agriculture and allied interests and fisheries), of whom four at least are elected from each sub-panel;

Table 2: Seanad General Elections 1965-77, number of candidates nominated and elected from each sub-panel

Panel	Cultural and Educational	Agricultural	Labour	Industrial and Commercial	Administrative
No. of Seats	5	11	11	9	7
Minimum from each sub-panel	2	4	4	3	3
1965					
Nominating bodies sub-panel					
nominated	13	12	11	12	7
elected	2	4	4	3	3
Oireachtas sub-panel					
nominated	5	13	9	10	9
elected	3	7	7	6	4
1969					
Nominating bodies sub-panel					
nominated	14	11	9	15	7
elected	2	4	4	3	3
Oireachtas sub-panel					
nominated	6	14	9	8	8
elected	3	7	7	6	4
1973					
Nominating bodies sub-panel					
nominated	17	14	9	20	8
elected	2	4	4	3	3
Oireachtas sub-panel					
nominated	5	12	9	8	9
elected	3	7	7	6	4
1977					
Nominating bodies sub-panel					
nominated	16	12	12	24	12
elected	2	4	4	3	3
Oireachtas sub-panel					
nominated	5	14	9	9	9
elected	3	7	7	6	4

3. eleven members from the labour panel (representing labour, whether organised or unorganised), of whom four at least are elected from each sub-panel;

4. nine members from the industrial and commercial panel (representing industry and commerce and including banking, finance, accountancy, engineering and architecture), of whom three at least are elected from each sub-panel;

5. seven members from the administrative panel (representing public administration and social services, including voluntary social activities), of whom three at least are elected from each sub-panel.

Table 2 (page 5) sets out the numbers nominated and elected for each sub-panel in the four general elections since 1965.

The register of nominating bodies* contains the names of those bodies whose aims are connected with the interests and services mentioned in the Constitution in respect of the various panels. The method of compilation and annual revision of the register and provisions relating to eligibility for registration are contained in sections 8 to 20 of the Seanad Electoral (Panel Members) Act, 1947, as amended by sections 3 to 6 of, and the schedule to, the Seanad Electoral (Panel Members) Act, 1954.

*See Appendix for composition of present register.

2 Eligibility for election

Every citizen without distinction of sex who has reached the age of twenty-one years, and who is not placed under disability or incapacity by the Constitution or by law, is eligible for membership of the Dáil and Seanad (Articles 16.1 and 18.2 of the Constitution).

Disability or incapacity may be divided into three categories:

1. *Constitutional incapacities*
Each of the following persons may not be a member of either House:

President of Ireland (Article 12.6.1°),
Comptroller and Auditor General (Article 33.3),
Any judge (Article 35.3).

No person may be at the same time a member of both Houses (Article 15.14).

2. *Legal disqualifications*
Section 51 (2) of the Electoral Act, 1923 provides that each of the following persons is disqualified from being elected to either House and from sitting as a member:
(1) a person who is undergoing a sentence of imprisonment with hard labour for any period exceeding six months or of penal servitude for any term imposed by a court of competent jurisdiction;
(2) an imbecile and any person of unsound mind;
3) an undischarged bankrupt under an adjudication by a court of competent jurisdiction;
(4) a person who is, because of the law relating to corrupt practices and other offences at elections, incapacitated from being a member because he has been found guilty by a court of competent jurisdiction of some such practice or offence.

7

3. *Legal incapacities*

Section 51 (3) of the Electoral Act, 1923 declares that a person shall be incapable of being elected or sitting as a member of either House who is:

(1) a member of the defence forces on full pay

(2) a member of any police force on full pay

(3) a person either temporarily or permanently in the civil service, unless he is by the terms of his employment expressly permitted to be a member of either House.

In addition, members of either House are disqualified from being members of boards of state-sponsored bodies, e.g. section 2 of the Central Bank Act, 1964; section 7 (7) of the Transport Act, 1950; section 9 (1) of the Electricity (Supply)' (Amendment) Act, 1958.

In regard to membership of the Seanad, the candidates for each panel must satisfy the Seanad returning officer that they have knowledge and practical experience of the interests and services represented on the panel (section 36 of the Seanad Electoral (Panel Members) Act, 1947). The section further provides (subsection (3)) that the returning officer shall have due regard to all decisions of the judicial referee (President of High Court or some other judge of the High Court nominated by him as set down in section 38 of the same Act) on questions referred to him under the Act, e.g. a question of doubt relating to a person's eligibility for nomination because of statutory incapacity or disqualification may be referred to the judicial referee for his decision on the point of law involved, and the returning officer then decides whether the nomination is in order or not.

3 Electorate

Dáil Éireann

Every citizen without distinction of sex who has reached the age of eighteen years, is not disqualified by law, and who complies with the provisions of the law relating to the election of members of the Dáil has the right under the Constitution (Article 16.1.2°) to vote at an election. Members are elected on the system of proportional representation by means of the single transferable vote (Article 16.2.5°).

The Electoral Acts provide that a person shall be entitled to be registered as a Dáil elector in a constituency if he has reached the age of eighteen years and was, on the qualifying date, ordinarily resident in that constituency and a citizen of Ireland. The Fourth Amendment of the Constitution Bill, 1972 which provides for the reduction of the minimum age to eighteen, was passed at a referendum on 6 December 1972. It is the duty of the county councils and county borough corporations to compile the register of electors which is subject to adjudication by county registrars on claims for and objections to the entry of names in the register (sections 6 and 7 of the Electoral Act, 1963).

No voter may exercise more than one vote, and the voting is by secret ballot (Article 16.1.4°) of the Constitution). Postal voting at elections to the Dáil is confined to members of the Garda Síochána and full-time members of the Defence Forces (section 7 of the Electoral Act, 1963).

Seanad Éireann

Section 44 of the Seanad Electoral (Panel Members) Act, 1947 provides that the electorate for the forty-three members of the Seanad elected from panels of candidates shall consist of:

9

1. the members of the Dáil (elected at the Dáil election consequent on the dissolution of the Dáil which occasioned the Seanad general election)
2. the members of the Seanad
3. the members of every council of a county or county borough.

If a person is a member of the electorate by virtue of more than one of these qualifications his name is entered once only on the electoral roll.

The electorate for bye-elections for casual vacancies among the panel members consists only of the members of the Dáil and the members of the Seanad who at a date prior to polling day are then entitled to sit and vote in their respective Houses (section 69 of the Seanad Electoral (Panel Members) Act, 1947).

Section 7 of the Seanad Electoral (University Members) Act, 1937 (as amended by section 3 of the Seanad Electoral (University Members) Act, 1973) provides that the electorate for the six members of the Seanad elected from the universities shall consist in the case of the National University of Ireland, of every Irish citizen who has received a degree (other than an honorary degree) in the university and has reached the age of eighteen years, and in the case of the University of Dublin, of every Irish citizen who has received a degree (other than an honorary degree) in the university or has obtained a foundation scholarship in the university or, if a woman, has obtained a non-foundation scholarship, and (in any case) has attained the age of eighteen years.

Every election is held on the system of proportional representation by means of the single transferable vote and by secret postal ballot (Article 18.5 of the Constitution). There is a separate election for each panel and for each of the universities.

4 Nomination of candidates

Dáil Éireann

A person may nominate himself as a candidate for election to the Dáil or may, with his consent, be nominated by another person who is registered as a Dáil elector in the constituency for which he proposes to nominate the candidate (section 21 of the Electoral Act, 1963).

The Electoral Act, 1963 provides for the establishment and maintenance of a formal register of political parties. The registrar is the Clerk of the Dáil. A candidate is permitted to include in his nomination paper the name of the registered political party he represents or, if he does not represent a party, to describe himself as 'non-party'. The particulars will then appear on the ballot papers at an election (sections 13, 16, 21 and Second Schedule).

Seanad Éireann

At an election for panel members a candidate may be nominated either by:
1. four members of the Houses of the Oireachtas (section 25 of the Seanad Electoral (Panel Members) Act, 1947), or by
2. a registered nominating body (section 26 of the Seanad Electoral (Panel Members) Act, 1947).

The names of the candidates nominated by members of the Houses to a panel eventually comprise the Oireachtas sub-panel of the panel; lists of the nominations by the nominating bodies to the panel ultimately comprise the nominating bodies sub-panel.

A member of either House may not join in the nomination of more than one person. Registered nominating bodies for a particular panel are entitled to propose for nomination the

11

number of persons provided for by section 26 of the Seanad Electoral (Panel Members) Act, 1947, as amended by the Act of 1954.

At bye-elections for casual vacancies among the panel members a candidate may be nominated either by:

1. nine members of the Houses of the Oireachtas (section 67 of the Seanad Electoral (Panel Members) Act, 1947), or by

2. a registered nominating body (section 59 of the Seanad Electoral (Panel Members) Act, 1947, as amended by the Act of 1954).

The choice of nominator is determined by whether the vacancy has occurred among senators elected from the Oireachtas sub-panel, or from the nominating bodies sub-panel of the particular panel.

At an election (including a bye-election) for university members, candidates are nominated in writing by two registered electors of the university as proposer and seconder respectively, and by eight other registered electors who assent to the nomination (section 16 of the Seanad Electoral (University Members) Act, 1937).

5 Duration, dissolution and membership of the Houses

Dáil Éireann

Article 16.5 of the Constitution provides that the same Dáil Éireann shall not continue for a longer period than seven years from the date of its first meeting and that a shorter period may be fixed by law. A maximum period of five years has been fixed by section 10 of the Electoral Act, 1963.

Article 13.2.1° of the Constitution provides that Dáil Éireann shall be summoned and dissolved by the President on the advice of the Taoiseach. Article 13.2.2° provides that the President may, in his absolute discretion, refuse to dissolve the Dáil on the advice of a Taoiseach who has ceased to retain the support of a majority in the Dáil. To date, this discretionary power has not been invoked by a President.

The proclamation issued by the President pursuant to the provisions of Article 13.2 sets out, inter alia, the date of dissolution of the outgoing Dáil and the date on which the new Dáil will meet. The Constitution (Article 16.3.2°) provides that a general election for membership of the Dáil shall take place not later than thirty days after a dissolution and (Article 16.4.2°) that the newly-elected Dáil shall meet within thirty days from the polling date. The date of the poll is appointed by order of the Minister for the Environment pursuant to section 24 of the Electoral Act, 1963.

Section 12 of the Electoral Act, 1963 provides that, immediately upon the issue of the Presidential proclamation dissolving the Dáil, the Clerk of the Dáil shall issue his writ, in the form set out in Part I of the Second Schedule to the Electoral Act, 1963, to the returning officer (sheriff or county registrar — see section 11 of the Electoral Act, 1963) in each constituency, directing him to cause an election to be held of the full number of members of the Dáil to serve for

13

his constituency. The present constituencies and the number of members for each constituency are set out in the Schedule to the Electoral (Amendment) Act, 1974.

Pursuant to Article 16.6 of the Constitution, provision is made by section 14 of the Electoral Act, 1963, to enable the outgoing Ceann Comhairle (Chairman), if he so desires, to be deemed to be elected to the new Dáil for the constituency for which he was a member immediately before the dissolution.

The rules for the conduct of elections to the Dáil are set out in detail in the Third, Fourth and Fifth Schedules to the Electoral Act, 1923, as amended by the Electoral Act, 1963.

When the count is completed, the returning officer endorses on the writ the names of the members returned for the constituency, and forwards it to the Clerk of the Dáil (section 12 of the Electoral Act, 1963). A newly-elected member is notified by the Clerk to attend and sign the roll of members provided for in the standing orders. The Clerk, at the first meeting of the House subsequent to the election, makes a report pursuant to standing orders, about the issue of writs for the election and announces to the House the names and constituencies of all the members returned to serve in it.

In the case of a bye-election, the Dáil, in accordance with standing orders, passes a resolution directing the Ceann Comhairle to direct the Clerk to issue his writ for election of a member to fill the vacancy. Otherwise the procedure is the same as that for a general election.

An elected candidate is a member of the Dáil from the date of his election to the date on which the Dáil is dissolved. On signing the roll of members, he becomes entitled to take his seat. A member of the Dáil ceases to be a member if he dies, resigns or is disqualified before the dissolution of the Dáil.

Pursuant to Article 28.11.2° of the Constitution, the members of the government in office at the date of the dissolution of the Dáil continue to hold office until their successors have been appointed.

Attendance at Dáil debates is not compulsory and no official record is kept of the members attending. If a member is suspended from the Dáil for disregarding the authority of the Chair, his suspension on the first occasion continues until the fourth day, on the second occasion until the eighth day, and on the third or any subsequent occasion until the twelfth day on which the Dáil shall sit after the day on which he was suspended. The order for suspension may be discharged by the House on receipt of a written and approved expression of regret from the member. Suspension of a member from the House does not exempt him from serving on a select or special committee to which he may previously have been appointed.

As from 1 March 1979 members are paid £6,911 per annum, subject to income tax. Each member of the House is granted travelling, postal and telephone facilities in connexion with his duties as a public representative. Travelling facilities mean (1) free first-class railway travel, (2) the repayment of fares paid on public transport, (3) the repayment of travelling expenses in the member's own motor car at sanctioned mileage rates, and (4) the repayment of any other moderate travelling expenses that are incurred. The travelling facilities granted generally include travelling between the member's constituency and Dublin, or, if the member does not reside in his constituency, between his place of residence and Dublin, between his place of residence and his constituency, and between Dublin and his constituency (Oireachtas (Allowances to Members) Acts, 1938, 1947 and 1962). An allowance of £10 per night is payable to a member who makes an overnight stay in accordance with the provisions of the Oireachtas (Allowances to Members) Act, 1962.

As from 1 March 1979 salaries payable for ministerial and parliamentary offices are as follows: Taoiseach £12,104 a year; Tánaiste £8,905 a year; other members of the government £8,101 a year; Ministers of State £5,207 a year; Chairman of Dáil Éireann £8,101 a year; Deputy Chairman of Dáil Éireann £4,098 a year. In each case, the amounts are additional to the allowance paid to the member as a deputy.

The leaders of parties of prescribed numerical strength are paid allowances for expenses (including expenses incurred in respect of research) in accordance with the following statutory formula:

1. Where there is one qualified party which is a government party and not more, there shall be paid to the leader of that party an annual sum of £20,205.

2. Where there are two qualified parties both of which are government parties and not more —

   (1) there shall be paid to the leader of that one of those qualified parties which is of the greater numerical strength in Dáil Éireann an annual sum of £14,143.

   (2) there shall be paid to the leader of the other such qualified party an annual sum of £6,062.

3. Where there are three or more qualified parties all of which are government parties —

   (1) there shall be paid to the leader of that one of those qualified parties which is of the greatest numerical strength in Dáil Éireann an annual sum of £10,103.

   (2) there shall be paid to each of the leaders of the other such qualified parties an annual sum of £10,103 divided by the number of the other such qualified parties.

4. Where there is one qualified party which is not a government party and not more, there shall be paid to the leader of that party an annual sum of £50,524.

5. Where there are two qualified parties neither of which is a government party and not more —

   (1) there shall be paid to the leader of that one of those qualified parties which is of the greater numerical strength in Dáil Éireann an annual sum of £45,365.

   (2) there shall be paid to the leader of the other such qualified party an annual sum of £20,158.

6. Where there are three or more qualified parties none of which is a government party —

   (1) there shall be paid to the leader of that one of those qualified parties which is of the greatest numerical strength in Dáil Éireann an annual sum of £25,262.

   (2) there shall be paid to each of the leaders of the other such qualified parties an annual sum of £25,262 divided by the number of the other qualified parties.

Seanad Éireann

Article 18.8 of the Constitution provides that a general election for the Seanad shall take place not later than ninety days after a dissolution of Dáil Éireann, and that the first meeting of the new Seanad, after the general election, shall take place on a day to be fixed by the President on the advice of the Taoiseach.

The Minister for the Environment makes orders within seven days after the dissolution of the Dáil setting out the dates and times at which the various procedures for the election of the panel members and university members of the Seanad are to take place (section 24 of the Seanad Electoral (Panel Members) Act, 1947, and section 12 of the Seanad Electoral (University Members) Act, 1937).

The returning officer for the election of the panel members is, by virtue of section 4 of the Seanad Electoral (Panel Members) Act, 1947, the Clerk of the Seanad. The returning officer for the National University is the Vice-Chancellor, and for Dublin University the Provost (section 14 of the Seanad Electoral (University Members) Act, 1937).

The rules for the conduct of the elections are set out in the schedules to the acts referred to above as amended by the Electoral Amendment Act, 1973. The returning officers for the university constituencies forward certificates to the Clerk of the Seanad containing, inter alia, the names of the candidates elected. The names of the members nominated by the Taoiseach pursuant to Article 18.3 of the Constitution are communicated to the Clerk by the Department of the Taoiseach. The members of the new Seanad are notified by the Clerk to attend and sign the roll of members provided for in the standing orders. At the first meeting of the House subsequent to a general election, the Clerk announces, pursuant to standing orders, the names of the members who have been nominated and elected respectively.

When a vacancy occurs in the number of members of the Seanad nominated by the Taoiseach, the Chairman, pursuant to standing orders, sends a notice of the vacancy in writing to the Taoiseach. The Taoiseach then nominates a person to fill the vacancy. When a vacancy occurs among the elected members, the Clerk, by direction of the Seanad, sends a notice of the vacancy in writing to the Minister for the Environment, who makes an order similar to that made by him for a general election. The method of election and subsequent procedure is similar to that for a general election except that there is a restricted electorate for a panel vacancy (see page 10).

Every member of Seanad Éireann, unless he dies, resigns or becomes disqualified, continues to hold office until the day before the polling day of the Seanad general election held after his election or nomination (Article 18.9).

Attendance in the Seanad is not compulsory and no official record is kept of the members attending. If a member is suspended from the Seanad by the Chair for disregarding the authority of the Chair, his suspension on the first occasion continues for one week, on the second occasion for a fortnight and on the third or any subsequent occasion for one month. The order for suspension may be discharged by the House on receipt of a written and approved expression of regret from the member. Suspension of a member from the House does not exempt him from serving on a select or special committee to which he may previously have been appointed.

As from 1 March 1979 members are paid £4,068 per annum subject to income tax. Each member of the House is granted travelling, postal and telephone facilities, and overnight subsistence allowances in connexion with his duties as a public representative. The facilities are similar to those granted to members of the Dáil and include travelling expenses between Dublin and the member's residence. The Chairman of the Seanad receives a salary of £3,447 per annum and the Deputy Chairman £1,843 per annum, in addition to their allowances as senators.

Privileges of members

Under the Constitution (Article 15.13), the members of each House are, except in case of treason, felony or breach of the peace, privileged from arrest within the precincts of either House and when going to and returning from either House; they are not, in respect of any utterance in either House, amenable to any court or any authority other than the House itself.

Each House, pursuant to Article 15.10, makes its own rules and standing orders, and has powers to attach penalties for their infringement, to ensure freedom of debate, to protect its official documents and the private papers of its members, and to protect itself and its members against any person or persons interfering with, molesting or attempting to corrupt its members in the exercise of their duties.

All official reports and publications of the Oireachtas or of either House, and utterances made in either House, wherever published, are privileged (Article 15.12).

The Committees of the Houses of the Oireachtas (Privilege and Procedure) Act, 1976 provides that a member of either House shall not, in respect of any utterance in or before a committee appointed by either House or jointly by both Houses, be amenable to any court or any authority other than the House or Houses by which the committee was appointed. The Act also provides that (1) the documents of a committee and the documents of its members connected with the committee or its functions, (2) all official reports and publications of a committee, and (3) the utterances in a committee of the members, advisers, officials and agents of the committee, wherever published, shall be privileged.

6 Powers of the Houses: general

The Upper House (Seanad) in Ireland, does not have all the prerogatives and powers of the Lower House (Dáil) and this is the case in most unitary states. In such states, almost all Upper Houses are appointed by a complex voting system which involves election by indirect suffrage by means of a restricted electoral college. This system is partly explained by the role of these Houses. Their function is a minor one and is confined to general debates and to proposing amendments for the consideration of the lower Houses.

In most federal states, such as the USA, the Federal Republic of Germany, and Switzerland, the Upper House has a completely different role. In these countries, it represents (usually on the basis of equal representation for each constituent element irrespective of population) the federated states which comprise the federation, and is almost always elected — in most cases by direct suffrage. In such states, each House may have special rights which, though not identical to those of the other chamber, put it in a position of substantial equality. In the USA, for example, the House of Representatives has the sole power of impeachment and the sole right to initiate legislation on revenue; the United States Senate has the sole right to confirm or reject Presidential appointments and to concur in treaties. However, the Dáil and Seanad have equal and/or complementary powers in regard to the following:

1. The Chairmen of both Houses are ex officio members of the Council of State (Article 31.2) and, with the Chief Justice, constitute under Article 14 the Commission which performs the powers and functions of the President in his absence.

2. The removal from office of the following:

(1) the President (Article 12.10)
(2) the Comptroller and Auditor General (Article 33.5), and
(3) a judge of the Supreme Court or of the High Court (Article 35.4). (A similar power is vested in both Houses in the case of a Circuit Court judge by virtue of section 39 of the Courts of Justice Act, 1924 and in the case of a justice of the District Court by virtue of section 20 of the Courts of Justice (District Court) Act, 1946.)

These persons cannot be removed from office except for stated misbehaviour or incapacity and their removal requires resolutions of both Houses.

3. The declaration and termination of a state of emergency requires resolutions of both Houses (Article 28.3.3°).

4. Initiation of bills, other than money bills and bills to amend the Constitution, the initiation of which is the constitutional prerogative of the Dáil (Articles 21.1 and 46.2).

5. The continuance in force of an Act for a period longer than ninety days, the time for the consideration of which as a bill was abridged, requires resolutions of both Houses. (Under Article 24 of the Constitution, the time for the consideration of a bill by the Seanad, which has been certified by the Taoiseach to be urgent and immediately necessary for the preservation of the public peace and security or because of the existence of a public emergency (domestic or international), may be abridged if the Dáil so resolves and if the President, after consultation with the Council of State, concurs. When enacted, it remains in force for ninety days after the date of its enactment unless both Houses agree to prolong the period.)

6. Annulment of statutory instruments under various statutes. (See also the section *Statutory Instruments Committee* in Chapter 10.)

The Seanad has prior or exclusive powers in relation to the following:

1. When a bill which is rejected by the Seanad or passed by it with amendments to which the Dáil does not agree (or which is neither passed nor rejected by the Seanad within ninety days from its receipt from the Dáil), a majority of the members of the Seanad and one-third of the members of the Dáil may, pursuant to Article 27 of the Constitution, jointly

petition the President to decline to sign the bill and promulgate it as a law because it contains a proposal of such national importance that the will of the people ought to be ascertained. If the President, after consultation with the Council of State, decides to accept the petition, the bill must be approved by the people at a referendum or by resolution of a new Dáil within eighteen months of the decision, before it may be signed and promulgated. No case has arisen under this provision.

2. The certificate of the Ceann Comhairle under Article 22.2 of the Constitution, that a bill is a money bill, may be challenged by a resolution of the Seanad requesting the President to refer the question to a Committee of Privileges consisting of an equal number of members of both Houses and a judge of the Supreme Court as chairman. If the President accedes to the request, the matter is determined finally and conclusively by the Committee. No case has arisen under this provision.

3. The President may sign a bill earlier than the fifth day after the date on which it is presented to him at the request of the government, with the prior concurrence of the Seanad (Article 25.2.2°). This occurs comparatively frequently, e.g. in case of bills which have to be enacted by a specified date.

4. Initiation of private bills (pursuant to standing orders relating to private business).

The relatively superior powers of the Dáil may be appropriately considered under three headings: control over the executive, the finances of the state, and legislation. The procedure of the Houses in dealing with the three elements are outlined in some detail in the following chapters.

7 Powers of the Houses: control over the Executive

Under the Constitution (Article 28.4.1°), the government is responsible to the Dáil alone. This responsibility pertains to the right of the Dáil to nominate the Taoiseach, to approve of the nomination by the Taoiseach of the other members of the government and, when the government is appointed by the President, to examine and criticise its administration.

Appointments of the Taoiseach and other Members of the Government

Article 13.1.1° of the Constitution provides that the President shall, on the nomination of the Dáil, appoint the Taoiseach. The President, on the nomination of the Taoiseach and with the prior approval of the Dáil, appoints the other members of the government (Article 13.1.2°). It is customary (though not mandatory) for the Taoiseach to inform the Dáil of the departments to which he has assigned the members of the government.

All members of the government, numbering not less than seven and not more than fifteen (Article 28.1), must be members of either House (Article 28.7). The Taoiseach, Tánaiste and Minister for Finance must be members of the Dáil and not more than two of the other members of the government may be members of the Seanad (Article 28.7).

From time to time the government may, on the nomination of the Taoiseach, appoint not more than ten members of the Houses of the Oireachtas to be Ministers of State and may at any time remove any Minister of State so appointed (section 1 of the Ministers and Secretaries (Amendment) (No. 2) Act, 1977).

Every member of the government has the right to attend and be heard in each House (Article 28.8). Ministers of State are accorded a similar right by the standing orders of both Houses.

The government meets and acts as a collective authority and is collectively responsible for the departments of state administered by its members (Article 28.4.2°).

The Constitution (Article 28.10) provides that the Taoiseach shall resign from office if he ceases to retain the support of a majority in the Dáil, unless on his advice (which is not necessarily accepted (Article 13.2.2°) the President dissolves the Dáil and the Taoiseach secures the support of a majority of the newly reassembled Dáil. The Taoiseach's resignation terminates the appointment of the other members of the government, but all members, including the Taoiseach, carry on their duties until their successors are appointed (Article 28.11).

It should be pointed out at this stage that the provisions relating to membership of the government, and the appointment and dismissal of governments, with which we are familiar in Ireland, are not necessarily common to all democratic countries. To take an extreme example: the executive in the United States is practically independent of both Houses of the Legislature, and members of the government are appointed by the President without any reference to the House of Representatives. However, these appointments require the consent of the Senate.

In the United Kingdom, although the government must depend on retaining the support of a majority in the House of Commons, neither the Prime Minister nor the other members of the government have to be formally nominated by the House.

Similarly, in other countries such as Australia and India, persons other than members of parliament may, at any rate initially, be appointed members of the government. In certain countries, members of parliament who are appointed ministers lose their rights in parliament (in Brazil, France and Switzerland for example) or even their seats, as in the USA. This latter requirement arises from what seems to Irish people a rather rigid application of the doctrine of the separation of the powers of the executive and the legislature.

The power of dissolution in Ireland, as in the United Kingdom, is one of the most important features that distinguishes this system from that in force in the USA and in many other countries. Its absence from the US system is a logical consequence of the separation there of the executive and legislative bodies, which for specified periods continue independently of each other.

In certain countries, such as Switzerland and Brazil, the executive cannot prematurely end the term of parliament by dissolution; in others, like Australia and the Federal Republic of Germany, dissolution is limited by legal or constitutional requirements. It may be noted that Article 12 of the French Constitution of October 1958 states that the President of the Republic may, after consultation with the Premier and the Presidents of the two Houses, dissolve the National Assembly. No further dissolution can take place within a year following the election of a new National Assembly. This is a stronger provision than the analogous one in the previous Constitution.

The power of dissolution, by or on the advice of the executive, acts as a powerful deterrent to capricious withdrawal of confidence by parliament. It has been frequently held that the absence or curtailment of such a power leads in many cases to frequent changes of government, and not always for compelling reasons.

Control of Administration

The Dáil has a number of exclusive constitutional responsibilities in connexion with executive action: to consider the estimates of receipts and expenditure of the state (Article 17.1), to approve international agreements involving charges upon public funds (Article 29.5.2°), and to assent to a declaration of or participation in war (Article 28.3.1°).

The most immediate control of public administration exercised by the Dáil is the parliamentary question. Members have the right to address questions to members of the government about public affairs connected with their departments or on matters of administration for which the members of the government are officially responsible. These questions are in writing and normally require three days notice. They are at present answered by the members of the government at sittings of the House on Tuesdays, Wednesdays and Thursdays from 2.30 p.m. to 3.30 p.m. A question relating to a matter of urgent public importance may, with the permission of the Ceann Comhairle, be asked on private notice to a member of the government (see for example, *Dáil Debates,* Vol. 264, Cols. 45/9 of 28/11/72). Ad hoc supplementary questions may be allowed, at the discretion of the Chair.

The Chair has no power to compel a member of the government to answer a question. Although members of the government normally have statutory authority to seek information concerning the activities of state-sponsored bodies, they generally refuse to answer questions relating to the day-to-day administration of these bodies and cannot be compelled by the Chair to do so. However, they may supply the required information, e.g. it is the practice to do so in the case of the Electricity Supply Board's rural electrification activities.

Members may also submit questions for written reply, and when the answers have been given they are printed in the official report. Questions cannot lead to a debate or to a vote; neither can the half-hour discussion on the adjournment which a member, who is dissatisfied with an answer, may initiate with the consent of the Chair. However, a matter to be raised on the adjournment in either House need not necessarily arise out of a question (it obviously never does in the Seanad where there is no provision for questions), nor is it automatically in order for the adjournment debate merely because it has been the subject of a question. The Chair, in the Dáil or Seanad, would not allow a matter to be raised for which a member of the government has no official responsibility: the Minister for Lands answers questions relating to the activities of the Land Commission, but they may not be pursued on the adjournment, since he is not officially responsible for the Commission's decisions. The Chair would also not allow discussion on a matter which involves the advocacy of legislation, which is sub judice, or which may more properly be brought forward as a substantive motion.

However, there is another form of motion on the adjournment which may give rise to a decision: a motion, submitted by a member to the Ceann Comhairle at the commencement of public business, to adjourn the House on a specific and important matter of public interest requiring urgent consideration. In the Dáil such a motion may be made if a member, who has given notice to the Ceann Comhairle before the opening of the sitting, rises in his place at the commencement of public business and states that he requests leave to move the adjournment of the Dáil in order to discuss a specific and important matter of public interest requiring urgent consideration. He then states the matter. If the Ceann Comhairle considers that the motion is one contemplated by the standing order, and not less than twelve members support it, he gives leave for the motion to be moved at 7 p.m. on a Tuesday or Wednesday, at 3.30 p.m. on a Thursday, or at such hour on the day the request is made that the Dáil appoints. A matter which fails to obtain the requisite support cannot be brought forward under the standing order again for the following six months.

A similar procedure exists in the Seanad. However, senators are not confined to initiating the procedure at the commencement of public business. They may utilise it by giving written private notice to the Cathaoirleach up to 2.30 p.m. on a day on which the Seanad meets before noon and up to 4.30 p.m. when the Seanad meets at or after noon. The number of members required to support the motion in the House is five and the Cathaoirleach fixes the hour (on the same day) at which the motion shall be moved.

Substantive motions, even though they do not relate to matters involving ministerial responsibility and despite the fact that they advocate legislation, may be put down by members of the Dáil, but they may not be discussed while their subject matter is sub judice. However, the standing orders provide that no member may reopen discussion on a question already discussed within the previous six months and also prohibit the discussion by way of anticipatory motions of matters already appointed for consideration. The Seanad procedure in relation to substantive motions is somewhat similar.

Four days notice of such motions is required. Motions or bills to be moved by private members of the Dáil are at present taken between 7 and 8.30 p.m. on Tuesdays and

Wednesdays, but a member of the government may move, without notice , at the commencement of public business that on that day or for a specified period government business be not interrupted. The number of hours devoted to this private members' business in the years 1969-78 are set out in Table 3 on p. 51. It must be remembered, however, that figures give a very incomplete picture of private members' rights, because during financial business they have an opportunity to speak on the estimates and to criticise administration; occasionally they have been allowed to discuss a motion relevant to the activities of the department or office concerned with an estimate. In recent years, government motions to approve policy decisions have occurred more frequently, thus allowing private members further opportunities for debate. Moreover, the parliamentary question is always available to deputies.

The standing orders of the Dáil provide for precedence to be given to private members' motions and bills. A party, which had not less than seven members elected at the previous general election (or all deputies who are not members of any party) constitutes a group which has the right to nominate in rotation a private member of the group, to move a motion in his name or to proceed with a stage of a bill in private members' time. The order by which the right is exercisable is determined by the number of members in the group, and larger groups have precedence over smaller ones. When there is an equal number of members, precedence is determined by lot. Each group also has the right to nominate one of its private members to present a bill (see p. 34-35) provided that there is not before the Dáil another bill presented by a member nominated by the group.

The nominated member gives notice to the Ceann Comhairle of the motion he proposes to move, or the stage of the bill to be taken, at least ten days prior to the date on which it is moved, and appropriate precedence is given to it in the private members' business on the Order Paper.

The time allowed for debate on a private member's motion, but not any stage of a private member's bill, is restricted to three hours in the Dáil and, for debate on the motion for second stage of a bill, to six hours (standing order 86). The speech of a member proposing a motion to which the time limit applies may not exceed forty minutes and he, or another member authorised by the proposer and who has not already spoken, is entitled to not less than fifteen minutes in reply. The speech of any other member participating in the debate may not exceed thirty minutes.

In the Seanad, pursuant to the resolution adopted on 7 December 1977, at least one motion other than government motions is taken each month if the exigencies of business allow. The time allowed is restricted to three hours, unless the House otherwise orders. The speech of the member proposing the motion may not exceed thirty minutes, and he, or another senator who is so authorised by the proposer and who has not already spoken, is entitled to fifteen minutes in reply. The speech of any other senator taking part in the debate may not exceed fifteen minutes.

8 Powers of the Houses: finances of the State

The Dáil has the superior constitutional authority in relation to the finances of the State, and the Seanad's duty concerning finance is limited to the consideration, within twenty-one days, of the bills giving legislative effect to financial proposals. For convenience, the procedure is outlined in chronological order.

The Constitution (Article 28.4.3°) states that the government shall prepare estimates of the receipts and estimates of the expenditure of the State in each financial year which for these purposes is now coextensive with the calendar year and shall present them to Dáil Éireann for consideration. It further provides (Article 17.1.1°) that, as soon as possible after their presentation, the Dáil shall consider the estimates. Standing Order 122 provides that the Estimates for Public Services shall be presented to the Dáil not less than seven days prior to the consideration of the ordinary yearly resolutions imposing taxation and not later than the thirtieth day of the financial year.

Pursuant to the constitutional directive, two documents known as the Estimates for Public Services and the Estimates of Receipts and Expenditure are presented to Dáil Éireann early each year. The Estimates for Public Services is a substantial volume giving detailed information of the estimates of expenditure on the supply services, which require to be approved each year. The Estimates of Receipts and Expenditure show in a concise form (1) the estimates of total expenditure for the financial year, (2) the estimates of receipts for the financial year based on the tax rates in force, and (3) the amounts of actual receipts and expenditure for the previous financial year. The estimates of total expenditure

30

in this document include the expenditure on the supply services, expenses on Central Fund services (i.e. those services not subject to annual vote, such as service of public debt, road fund, judicial salaries), and expenditure on capital and other issues. The Dáil is able to determine whether or not the Minister for Finance needs to procure additional moneys by taxation, borrowing or by some other means.

Estimates for Public Services

The Dáil discusses these Estimates individually or in related groups; it considers motions for granting sums for the services provided by the Estimates. To enable the public services to be financed during that part of the financial year when the Estimates for them are being considered, the Central Fund (Permanent Provisions) Act 1965 authorises the Minister for Finance to issue from the Central Fund an amount not exceeding four-fifths of the amount appropriated for each particular service during the preceding financial year and to use this sum to make good the supply for such services. The Act provides that any sum so issued shall be increased or reduced depending on the size of the supply eventually granted by the Dáil for the particular service. In December of each year, the Minister for Finance lays before the Dáil a statement of the sums which the Act authorises him to issue in the following financial year.

The debates on the Estimates comprehend both policy and the preceding year's administration. It is not permissible to criticise existing legislation or to advocate its amendment.

Under standing orders of the Dáil, only a member of the government may move a motion authorising expenditure (e.g. an estimate), a motion authorising a charge upon the people (e.g. taxation motion in connexion with the Budget), or an amendment to either one necessitating an increase in the amount named in any such motion. The basic constitutional provision in regard to expenditure provides (Article 17.2) that the Dáil shall not pass any vote or resolution, and no law shall be enacted, for the appropriation of revenue or other public moneys unless the purpose of the appropriation shall have been recommended to the Dáil by a message from the government signed by the Taoiseach. When all the Estimates have been agreed to, a bill is introduced to appropriate the total sum in the manner detailed in the schedule and this passes through the final stages in both Houses.

If, in the course of the year, it is discovered that the amount provided in the estimate is not sufficient or that a new service is required, a supplementary or additional estimate may be introduced by the appropriate member of the government. The debate on the supplementary vote is confined to the items constituting the vote and no discussion may take place on the original vote except in so far as it may be necessary to explain or illustrate the particular items under discussion.

If, however, expenditure in excess of the Estimate is not brought to notice until the expiry of the appropriate year, this expenditure requires an Excess Vote. The practice is to refer such Excess Votes to the Committee of Public Accounts and, on publication of its report, the Dáil considers the Votes (see, for instance, Interim Report T.209 of the Committee of Public Accounts of 8 June 1966 and *Dáil Debates,* Vol. 226, Col. 111, et seq.). The sums voted as a result of the supplementary estimate or Excess Vote are appropriated by the Appropriation Bill which is introduced after the Dáil has agreed to such estimate or vote.

Budget

The annual statement of the Minister for Finance, in which he submits his Estimates of Receipts and Expenditure for the current financial year, is made to the Dáil in January or February. In the statement, the Minister outlines, among other things, his proposals for new taxation and indicates the proposed changes to the existing tax structure. When he has concluded his statement, it is customary for a representative to make an ex tempore reply, on behalf of each opposition party, after which any financial motions (the terms of which are not disclosed until then) embodying the taxation proposals outlined by the Minister, are submitted to the Dáil for consideration.

Generally, it is considered necessary that financial resolutions imposing new taxation or varying existing taxation should, in the interests of revenue, be given statutory effect from the day upon which the proposals which they contain are made public. Therefore, the resolutions contain declarations that it is expedient that they should have statutory effect under the Provisional Collection of Taxes Act, 1927 as amended, normally for a period not exceeding four months from the date of operation. The practice is that the resolutions are passed on the day on which the Budget statement is made, the main debate on the Minister's statement being reserved for the final or general motion which is usually 'That it is expedient to amend the law relating to customs and inland revenue, and to make further provisions in connexion with Finance.'

The Finance Bill for the year, which is normally based upon financial resolutions, is introduced by the Minister for Finance as soon as practicable after the resolutions have been agreed to by the Dáil; its enactment gives the resolutions legislative effect.

9 Powers of the Houses: legislation

The Dáil has superior constitutional powers regarding legislation in the following instances:

1. A money bill, as defined in Article 22 of the Constitution, or a bill to amend the Constitution may be initiated only in that House. The Seanad has only twenty-one days to consider money bills and may make recommendations. It cannot amend them. If a money bill is not returned within twenty-one days, or is so returned with recommendations which the Dáil does not accept, it is deemed to have been passed by both Houses at the expiration of the twenty-one days;

2. Other bills, to which the Seanad does not agree, may be deemed to be passed by both Houses, pursuant to a resolution of the Dáil to that effect, within 180 days of the expiration of the ninety days period which the Seanad has for considering a bill (Article 23.1).

Bills may be divided into two main categories: public bills and private bills.

Public Bills

Public bills (with the exception of Consolidation Bills) go through five stages in the House in which they are initiated.

First Stage

A bill may be initiated in the Dáil by introduction or by presentation. The title of every bill to be introduced or presented and a short description of its purpose, prepared by the proposer and accepted by the Ceann Comhairle, appears on the Order Paper. In the case of introduction the member giving notice moves for leave to introduce the bill.

If this motion is opposed, the Ceann Comhairle, after permitting an explanatory statement not exceeding five minutes from the member who moves and from a member who opposes the motion, puts the question thereon. If permission is given to introduce the bill, an order is made for its consideration on second reading and the bill is printed. In the case of presentation a bill may be presented without previously obtaining the leave of the House and any bill so presented is printed and the House may then make an order for its consideration on second reading. A member of the government, a Minister of State or a private member nominated by his group may present a bill. A group, however, has the right to nominate a member to present a bill only provided that there is not before the Dáil another bill presented by a member nominated by the group. The Seanad has a similar procedure for presentation.

First stage is usually a formal stage agreed to without debate particularly in the case of government bills. It arises only in the initiating House and when the bill has passed all stages in that House it is first considered on second stage in the other House.

A government bill is initiated in the Dáil by a member of the government or by a Minister of State.

In the Seanad, a government bill is initiated by the Leader of the House. In the case of private members' bills, the initiative is exercised by not less than three senators and the member whose name appears as first signatory on the bill moves for leave to introduce it.

It has been urged frequently that bills of an administrative or technical nature should normally be introduced in the Seanad to enable that House to proceed with its legislative business while the Dáil debates the estimates. This would obviate the situation that often arises at the end of July each year when the Seanad finds itself with a large number of bills to deal with after the Dáil has gone into recess.

Second Stage

The debate on the motion 'That the Bill be now read a second time' is confined to the general principle of the bill, since matters of detail are more appropriately dealt with at the next stage. It is permissible for members to raise matters that they feel could relevantly be included in the bill.

In the Dáil, two kinds of amendments may be made to the motion:

1. By omitting the word 'now' and adding at the end of the motion 'this day three months' or some other date.

2. By omitting all or some of the words after 'That' and substituting words stating some special reason against the second reading.

The second type of amendment is the only one that may be moved in the Seanad at this stage. If the second reading is agreed to, the bill is ordered to be considered in committee. This is usually a committee of the whole House but it may be a special or select committee. This contrasts with the practice in the British House of Commons where bills are invariably sent 'upstairs' to the standing committees. However, in the Dáil, a private member's bill which receives a second reading must be referred to a select or special committee.

Third (Committee) Stage

The bill is considered section by section in committee; amendments may be made, sections deleted and new sections inserted.

Amendments must be relevant to the subject matter of the bill and must not be in conflict with the principle of the bill as read a second time. An amendment must be directed to omitting, adding or substituting words but may not be equivalent to a direct negative (e.g. to delete a section, since the same result is obtained by voting against the question 'That the section stand part of the Bill') or inconsistent with a previous decision.

An amendment necessitating a charge on the people must be covered by a financial resolution to the bill. If such a resolution is fundamental, it should by standing order be agreed to by the Dáil prior to the introduction of the bill although the present Dáil has by resolution decided that such a resolution may be taken at any time prior to committee stage but, if it is incidental, it may be taken at any time prior to the committee stage. An amendment to increase expenditure or a charge may be moved only by a member of the government or a Minister of State.

In the Seanad, government amendments are proposed from the Chair or moved by a senator who is a member of the government.

In committee, a member may speak more than once on the same question. When the sections have been disposed of, the schedules, the preamble (if any), and the long title to the bill are considered and amended, if this is necessary. The bill is then reported with or without amendment to the House and an order is made for its consideration on report. Variations in this procedure are permissible if they are authorised by instructions from the House.

A special committee deals with the bill in the same way as the committee of the whole House, whereas a select committee normally has power to send for persons, papers and records to take oral and written evidence. A bill reported from a select committee with power to send for persons, papers and records must, under the standing orders, be recommitted to a committee of the whole House. A special committee merely reports the bill with or without amendments, whereas a select committee may report in addition its opinions and observations and any minutes of evidence given before it.

The special committee procedure is the normal way to deal with private members' bills (see p. 39) and those government bills that are not dealt with in committee on the floor of the House: Defence Bill, 1951, Factories Bill, 1956, Companies Bill, 1962. The government bills sent to such committees have usually been those of a technical or consolidating nature. The select committee procedure is used mainly in the case of private bills, since it facilitates the hearing of counsel and the examination of witnesses, (see p. 40). This procedure is mandatory under standing orders relating to private business.

Fourth (Report) Stage

Amendments may be made at this stage. Amendments previously rejected in committee may not be moved, nor may amendments be moved which create a charge on the public revenue or upon the people, unless the House decides to recommit the bill in respect of them. In general, permissible amendments are drafting and minor amendments and those that substantially arise out of the proceedings of the committee. Debate on this stage is usually confined to any amendments which are moved. In the Dáil, when the amendments have been disposed of, an order for the fifth stage is made. In the Seanad, however, when the amendments have been disposed of, the question 'That the Bill (or the Bill, as amended) be received for final consideration' is decided and an order for the fifth stage is made.

Fifth Stage
On this stage, a general debate on the contents of the bill is permissible, but only verbal amendments may be made. The question proposed on ordinary (i.e. non-money) bills in each House is 'That the Bill do now pass' but, in the case of a money bill, the question proposed in the Seanad is 'That the Bill be returned to the Dáil'. When a bill is passed and has been sent to the other House, it is deemed to have passed its first stage in that House and is set down for its second stage. When the Seanad passes a Dáil bill with amendments, the Dáil considers these in committee. If the Dáil does not agree with all or any of the Seanad amendments, the matter is reconsidered by the Seanad which may decide whether or not to insist on the amendments. If it decides to insist, the provisions of Article 23.1.1° of the Constitution apply (see p. 34).

If a Seanad bill is amended in the Dáil, it is deemed to be a bill initiated in the Dáil (Article 20.2.2°) and is put down in the Seanad, pursuant to standing orders, for its fourth stage, and considered on that and the fifth stage only.

A bill which lapses before it has reached its final stage, because of the dissolution of the Dáil, may be dealt with on the reassembly of the Dáil at the stage it had reached prior to the dissolution; a resolution of the Dáil restoring it to the Order Paper is necessary. The bill is proceeded with at the commencement of the particular stage which it had reached prior to the dissolution, unless the resolution directs otherwise. A similar procedure may be adopted by the Seanad.

When a bill, other than a bill to amend the Constitution, is passed or deemed to have been passed by both Houses, it is sent to the President for his signature and promulgation as law (Article 25.1). The President signs the bill not earlier than the fifth day and not later than the seventh day after the date on which the bill is presented to him, unless a motion requesting his earlier signature is agreed to by the Seanad (Article 25.2) (see p. 22), or unless he decides to refer the bill to the Supreme Court (Article 26) or to a referendum (Article 27) (see p. 22). A bill to amend the Constitution which is passed or deemed to have been passed by both Houses and is approved of at a referendum (Article 47) is signed forthwith by the President (Article 46.5).

Consolidation Bills

A Consolidation Bill is a bill which is certified by the Attorney General as not containing substantive amendment of the law; it may be introduced in either House, but is invariably initiated in the Seanad. After receiving a second reading, it is referred to the Standing Joint Committee on Consolidation Bills (see Chapter 10) which reports it with or without amendment to both Houses.

The bill is then considered on the fourth and fifth stages in the initiating House and is then sent to the other House where the first, second and third stages are waived and it is considered on the fourth and fifth stages only. It is then enacted in the same way as an ordinary bill.

Private Members' Bills

A private member's bill is a public bill initiated by a member who is not a member of the government or a Minister of State. The procedure for the initiation of bills has been described on pages 34 and 35.

If a motion for leave to introduce such a bill is opposed in the Dáil, the debate is adjourned until the next Tuesday or Wednesday on which private members' business is taken.

The second stage of a private member's bill is taken in private members' time and, if agreed to, the bill is referred to a special or select committee. Bills involving incidental expenditure or taxation cannot proceed beyond the second stage without the appropriate message of recommendation from the government to the expenditure or the appropriate resolution of the Dáil opposing the taxation. Bills introduced by private members can be 'killed' at that stage if they are not approved of by the government. Only very rarely, however, will they proceed even so far. The final stages are also taken in private members' time.

In the Seanad, a private member's bill proceeds in the same way as a government bill.

During the Twentieth Dáil (March 1973 to May 1977), three bills were presented by private members; one was withdrawn, one negatived and one lapsed with the dissolution. The chances of a private member's bill reaching the statute book are remote, for even when the government accepts the principle of the bill, the member is normally requested to withdraw it on the assurance that the government will introduce a measure officially drafted to meet his case.

In the same period five bills were introduced in the Seanad; two were withdrawn, two were negatived and one lapsed with the dissolution.

Private Bills

Private bills are those promoted for the particular interest or benefit of any person or locality, as distinct from measures of public policy.

A private bill is, by virtue of the standing orders relating to private business, introduced in the Seanad after examination by the Examiner of Private Bills, (an officer appointed jointly by the Chairmen of the Houses), to ensure compliance with standing orders regarding advertising, notification to people or bodies affected thereby and departments of state (see Chapter 10). After the second reading has been agreed to by the Seanad, the bill is referred to a joint committee of both Houses consisting of a chairman nominated by the Chairmen of the Houses, three deputies and three senators who have no personal interest in the bill and also in the case of deputies whose constituents have no local interest in it.

The joint committee considers the bill, takes evidence, hears counsel on behalf of the promoters and objectors, considers reports from departments of state and reports the bill with or without amendments to both Houses.

Subsequently, the fourth and fifth stages are taken in the Seanad and the bill is sent to the Dáil where it is considered on fourth and fifth stages only, the other three stages being waived. It is then enacted in the same way as a public bill.

Fees on scales set out in the standing orders relative to private business are payable by the promoters and opponents of private bills.

10 Committees

No review of the functions of the Houses of the Oireachtas would be complete without reference to the committees set up by them and, an outline of the work which they do.

Ireland's system of committees is based on the British model and contrasts with the complicated system to be found, for example, in the USA and France whereby legislation is divided into distinct categories and each category is allocated to a standing committee. In the House of Representatives in the USA there are separate committees on ways and means, on appropriations, on the judiciary, on foreign affairs etc., and in the Senate, committees on foreign relations and commerce etc. All proposed legislation is referred to the particular committee which has special cognisance of the subject on which it is proposed to legislate. It reports the legislation with or without amendments, or adversely, or not at all to the parent House.

Under the Irish system, a committee does not make final decisions. It reports to the House which then decides. A special committee on a bill (corresponding to the standing committee in Britain) is a miniature of the committee of the whole House and is likely to judge the bill referred to it in the same way as the House would, thus relieving the House of the burden of committee work.

However, a select committee is normally set up to perform work for which the House is unsuited. Its type of investigation, which requires detailed inquiry, the examination of witnesses and the weighing of their evidence, is not one that a large assembly could conveniently perform. A bill reported from a select committee is recommitted to a committee of the whole House which has the advantage of having before it the report of the select committee containing its findings and opinions on the matters at issue, based on the expert advice to which it has had access.

At the commencement of every Dáil and Seanad, the Committees of Selection and the Committees on Procedure and Privileges are appointed.

Committee of Selection

This committee at present consists of thirteen members in the Dáil with a quorum of five, and eleven members, including the Leas-Chathaoirleach (Chairman ex officio), in the Seanad with a quorum of four. It nominates the members to serve on select or special committees, has power to discharge such members from time to time for non-attendance or at their own request, and to appoint others to replace those discharged. The committee, in common with other committees of the Houses, is so constituted as to be impartially representative of the House. The number of members on this committee and others which are provided for in the standing orders has been varied occasionally to ensure compliance with the latter requirements.

Committee on Procedure and Privileges

This committee consists of seventeen members and the Ceann Comhairle (Chairman ex officio) with a quorum of eight in the Dáil, and of ten members and the Cathaoirleach (Chairman ex officio) and Leas-Chathaoirleach with a quorum of five in the Seanad. It has power to consider matters of procedure, to recommend any additions or amendments to the standing orders and to consider and report on members' privileges.

The Dáil Committee may also consider any matter relating to the conditions or premises in which members carry out their duties which is not specifically referred to any other committee.

Joint Committees

The following joint committees of both Houses are nominated by the Committee of Selection:

44   *The Houses of the Oireachtas*

Joint Library Committee: consisting usually of seven members of each House with two from each as quorum, assists and advises the Ceann Comhairle and the Cathaoirleach in the direction and control of the Oireachtas Library.

Joint Restaurant Committee: constituted in the same way as the Library Committee, directs and controls the Oireachtas Restaurant.

Joint Committee on Standing Orders (Private Business): consists of three members of each House and a chairman nominated by the Ceann Comhairle and Cathaoirleach jointly (this position traditionally alternates between Leas-Cheann Comhairle and Leas-Chathaoirleach), with a quorum of three (at least one from each House). It nominates the members to serve on joint committees on private bills and can discharge and replace them.

It also considers reports from the Examiner of Private Bills that the standing orders have not been complied with by the promoters of these bills or as to the construction of standing orders and recommends whether they ought to be dispensed with and, if so, on what conditions.

Joint Committee on Consolidation Bills: consists of three members of each House, with two from each as quorum, and the member of the government responsible for the bill or on his nomination the appropriate Minister of State. The committee considers Consolidation Bills referred to it. It has power to send for persons, papers and records, and reports the bill with or without amendments and its observations on it to both Houses.

Joint Committee on the Secondary Legislation of the European Communities: The original committee was set up in 1973 after Ireland joined the European Communities. The present committee (appointed in 1977) consists of eighteen members of the Dáil and eight members of the Seanad with a quorum of five (at least one from each House). The committee examines such of the following as it selects and reports thereon to the Houses:
1. programmes and guidelines prepared by the Commission of the European Communities as a basis for possible legislative action and drafts of regulations, directives, decisions, recom-

mendations and opinions of the Council of Ministers proposed by the Commission;

2. acts of the institutions of the Communities;

3. regulations under the European Communities Act, 1972, and

4. other instruments made under statute and necessitated by the obligations of membership of the Communities.

Joint Committee on State Sponsored Bodies: The committee consists of seven members of the Dáil and four members of the Seanad (none of whom shall be a member of the government or a Minister of State), with a quorum of four (at least one from each House). The Committee examines (and reports thereon to the Houses) the reports and accounts and overall operational results of specified state sponsored bodies engaged in trading or commerical activities and in the case of one body, Gaeltarra Éireann, the trading and/or commercial aspects of the reports and accounts and its overall operational results. The committee has power to send for persons, papers and records and (subject to consent of the Minister for the Public Service) to engage the services of persons with specialist or technical knowledge to assist it for the purposes of particular enquiries.

Select Committees

Committee of Public Accounts: provides the last link in the chain of Dáil control over the finances of the state. It is appointed as soon as may be after the beginning of each financial year to examine and report to the Dáil upon the accounts which show the appropriation of the sums granted by the Dáil to meet public expenditure, and to suggest alterations and improvements in the form of the estimates submitted to the House. The annual report of the Comptroller and Auditor General containing his observations on the accounts, is referred to the committee to facilitate its work.

The Comptroller and Auditor General is appointed by the President on the nomination of the Dáil (Article 33.2 of the Constitution). He controls all disbursements on behalf of the state and audits all accounts of moneys administered by or under the authority of the Oireachtas (Article 33.1). Pursuant to Article 33.4, he reports to the Dáil at stated periods determined by law (see Exchequer and Audit Departments Acts, 1866 and 1921, as adapted by the Comptroller and Auditor General Act, 1923, for particulars of duties and reports). Like a judge, he can be removed from office only for stated misbehaviour or incapacity, after resolutions have been passed by both Houses calling for his removal.

The committee, which is nominated by the Committee of Selection, usually consists of twelve members, none of whom may be a member of the government or a Minister of State, and has a quorum of four. Traditionally, the chairman is a member of the opposition. The committee has power to send for persons, papers and records.

The appropriation account for each vote sets out the amount expended and the amount granted, and is signed by the accounting officer (the secretary of the department or head of the office) responsible for the vote. It is accompanied by a certificate of the Comptroller and Auditor General stating that the account is correct. When necessary, notes from the accounting officer are appended to the account explaining substantial variations between the amounts granted and the amounts spent.

The committee, in pursuance of its powers to send for persons, papers and records, examines the Comptroller and Auditor General, the accounting officers and officials of the Department of Finance, and their evidence is printed with the report of the committee. Supplementary written information from witnesses required by the committee is reproduced in appendixes to the report.

The investigations of the committee are made from a financial and not from a political point of view. It does not attempt any inquiry into matters of policy, which are determined by the Dáil: the amount of the estimates or the amount of any particular grant are matters of policy and it would be entirely outside the scope of the committee to question these or to investigate the ground on which they are based.

The Committee of Public Accounts reports to the Dáil. In practice these reports are rarely debated but are administratively dealt with by the Department of Finance which indicates to the committee by ministerial minute the steps it proposes to take to implement the committee's recommendations, or, if it disagrees with them, the reasons why. In the next ensuing year, the committee considers the finance minute on the report of the previous committee and if disagreements cannot be resolved, the Dáil, as final arbiter, decides the issue.

It is settled practice that an excess vote arising from over-expenditure of an estimate and supplementary estimates, if there are any, may not be submitted to the Dáil without having been previously considered by the committee. This is usually done at a meeting of the committee convened specifically for the purpose and its recommendations form the subject of an interim report.*

Committee on Statutory Instruments: This is a committee of Seanad Éireann which examines instruments made by the government or other bodies pursuant to statute and ensures that they comply with certain basic criteria set out in its terms of reference. The Seanad has equal powers with the Dáil to annul such orders. In fact, it may be argued that, in practice, the Upper House has superior powers, since the period of twenty-one sitting days during which an order is subject to annulment usually represents a considerably longer period in the life of the Seanad. Therefore, it was a natural development that that House would interest itself in the field of delegated legislation.

The committee was first constituted as a sessional committee (i.e. for the life of the House) in 1948 and has been similarly reconstituted since then at the commencement of every Seanad.

Its original terms of reference have been modified in detail and the committee, constituted in 1978 was set up pursuant to the following resolution of the Seanad:

1. that a Select Committee be appointed to consider every statutory instrument laid or laid in draft before Seanad Éireann in pursuance of a statutory requirement with a view to

*See Epitome of the Reports from the Committee of Public Accounts on the Appropriation Accounts from 1922-23 to 1933-34 and of the minutes of the Minister for Finance thereon, p. 88 et seq.

determining whether the special attention of Seanad Éireann should be drawn to it on any of the following grounds:

(1) that it imposes a charge on the public revenues or contains provisions requiring payments to be made to the exchequer or any government department or to any local or public authority in consideration of any licence or consent, or of any services to be rendered or prescribes the amount of any such charge or payments;

(2) that it appears to make some unusual or unexpected use of the powers conferred by the statute under which it is made;

(3) that it purports to have retrospective effect where the parent statute confers no express authority so to provide;

(4) that there appears to have been unjustifiable delay either in the laying of it before Seanad Éireann or in its publication;

(5) that its drafting appears to be defective; or

(6) that for any special reason its form or purport calls for elucidation;

or on any other ground which does not impinge on its merits or on the policy behind it; and to report accordingly;

2. that the committee consists of nine members of whom three shall form a quorum;

3. that the committee has power to require any government department or other instrument-making authority concerned to submit a memorandum explaining any statutory instrument which may be under its consideration or to depute a representative to appear before it as a witness for the purpose of explaining any such statutory instrument;

4. that the committee has power to report to Seanad Éireann from time to time any memoranda submitted or other evidence given to it in explanation of any statutory instrument;

5. that it be the duty of the committee before reporting that the special attention of Seanad Éireann should be drawn to any statutory instrument to afford to any government department or other instrument-making authority concerned therewith an opportunity of furnishing orally or in writing such explanations as the department or authority may think fit;

6. that every report which the committee proposes to make shall on adoption by the committee be laid before Seanad

Éireann forthwith whereupon the committee shall have power
to print and publish such report together with any memoranda
or evidence given to it in explanation of any statutory instrument.

The committee meets regularly and reports to the Seanad.
Its reports draw the attention of the House to the instruments
on the grounds set out in its terms of reference and also contains the minutes of evidence of witnesses summoned before
the committee and copies of the correspondence between the
committee and the departments or other instrument-making
authorities.

11 Sittings and business of the Houses

The Constitution (Article 15.7) provides that the Houses shall hold at least one session every year. Article 15.8 states that the sittings of each House shall be public, but, in cases of special emergency, either House may hold a private sitting with the assent of two-thirds of the members present (no such private sitting has yet been held). The average sittings of the Houses between 1969 and 1978 were 87 days per year for the Dáil, and 35 days per year for the Seanad. The greater proportion of sitting days in each House is in the period preceding the summer recess.

Dáil Éireann

The Dáil, unless it otherwise resolves, meets every Tuesday at 2.30 p.m. and every Wednesday and Thursday at 10.30 a.m., and adjourns not later than 9 p.m. on Tuesdays and Wednesdays and not later than 5.30 p.m. on Thursdays. However, the days and hours may be varied or extended, depending on the state of business in the House.

Every sitting of the Dáil is governed by a printed Order Paper which is prepared under the direction of the Ceann Comhairle. The Taoiseach has the right to determine the order in which government business shall appear on the Order Paper and he announces at the commencement of public business the order in which it is to be taken each day.

On Tuesdays, questions are answered normally at 2.30 p.m. and are first business. On Wednesdays and Thursdays, questions are taken during the sitting at 2.30 p.m. Second comes private business which relates to private bills and ancillary matters (to be distinguished from Private Members' Bills which are public bills introduced by private members). Then the House proceeds to deal with public business, including motions relating to the introduction of bills and orders of the day, i.e. business previously ordered by the House to be set down for that day.

On Tuesdays and Wednesdays, unless the House otherwise orders, private members' business is taken from 7 p.m. to 8.30 p.m.

The following table indicates the principal business transacted by the Dáil in the period 1969-1978 and the time devoted to financial business (estimates, budget debates and proposals for legislation consequential on them) and private members' business (apart from the occasional private members' motion taken in government time).

Table 3: Principal Business Transacted by the Dáil 1969-78

Year	Number of Dáil sittings	Total hours of sitting	Parliamentary questions		Financial business	Private members' business
			oral	written		
	(no.)	(hours)	(no.)	(no.)	(hours)	(hours)
1969	78	569	5,139	331	207	15
1970	89	712	5,270	291	286	1½
1971	99	835	6,056	499	366	27
1972	87	691	5,000	623	293	20
1973	65	493	3,585	458	247	—
1974	89	686	4,708	513	215	27
1975	110	979	4,324	870	234	63
1976	94	746	2,199	1,472	143	57
1977	76	563	2,380	2,031	79	60
1978	87	683	2,464	3,295	154	64

Seanad Éireann

The Seanad, unless it otherwise resolves, meets on Tuesdays at 2.30 p.m. and on Wednesdays and Thursdays at 10.30 a.m. Provision is made in the standing orders under which a meeting of the Seanad may be requisitioned on the written request of not less than thirty senators. There is also provision for postponing a meeting where the representatives of the groups in the Seanad so request.

The sittings of the Seanad are largely dependent on the volume of business sent to the House from the Dáil. While the Dáil is discussing the estimates, very little legislation is passed by it and the Seanad has no occasion to meet. The disparity in sittings between the two Houses is explained first by the difference in the number of members of each and, secondly, by the fact that debates similar to those in the Dáil on the Budget and the estimates do not take place in the Seanad.

Every sitting is governed by an Order Paper which is prepared under the direction of the Cathaoirleach.

The order of precedence of government bills, which form the greater proportion of the work of the Seanad, is decided by the Leader of the House after consultation with other interested parties. (The Leader of the House is a member of the House who supports the government and who moves motions for resolutions and bills on behalf of the government; non-members of the House, such as members of the government and Ministers of State, may not move motions in the House.) However, under standing orders, bills coming from the Dáil, other than money bills, and bills the time for the consideration of which by the Seanad shall have been abridged (Article 24 of the Constitution), cannot be considered before the expiration of three clear days after receipt from the Dáil, unless the Seanad otherwise orders.

The following table sets out the numbers and total hours of sittings of the Seanad in the period 1969-1978. Approximately 90-95 per cent of the work consisted of the consideration of legislation sent to the second chamber by the Dáil.

Table 4: Number and total hours of sittings of the Seanad,
1969-78

Year	Number of Seanad sittings	Total hours of sittings
	(no.)	(hours)
1969	22	136
1970	29	198
1971	47	332
1972	33	187
1973	22	149
1974	38	249
1975	63	466
1976	39	226
1977	25	134
1978	36	202

12 Powers and duties of Chairmen of the Houses

Article 15.9.1° of the Constitution provides that each House shall elect from its members its own Chairman and Deputy Chairman and shall prescribe their powers and duties.

Chairman of Dáil (Ceann Comhairle)

The standing orders of the Dáil devolve duties and confer authority upon the Chairman in matters concerning the conduct of proceedings and the general business and administration of the House.

The Chairman presides over the sittings of the Dáil and while doing so he is the sole judge of order. He calls on members to speak and all speeches must be addressed to him. He puts all questions that have to be put to the House, supervises divisions and declares the results of these. He has the authority to suppress disorder during the sitting and to enforce prompt obedience to his ruling, and he may order members to withdraw from the House or name them for suspension by the House for a specified period. He may adjourn the House if the proceedings become too disorderly. The Chairman has a wide variety of duties to do with the general business of the Dáil. The Order Paper which governs each sitting of the House is prepared under his direction. Each parliamentary question, motion or amendment which is tabled by a member is examined by him to ensure that it complies with the standing orders and precedents, and where it does not do so, he may disallow it or, after consultation with the member, amend it. It is within his discretion to accept questions, motions or amendments on shorter notice than that provided for in the standing orders and to accept during the course of a sitting certain formal motions relating to the sitting or its business. The Chairman is in control of and responsible for the administration (secretariat) of the Dáil. The minutes of proceedings of the House are perused and signed by him; when printed, these constitute the Journal of the Proceedings. The official Report of Debates is issued under his supervision. Under him and subject to his orders, the Clerk of the House has direction and control over all the officers and joint staff.

The Chairman is ex officio Chairman of the Committee on Procedure and Privileges of the Dáil.

Since the Chairman cannot physically preside over every sitting of the Dáil, the Deputy Chairman, when deputising, exercises the powers of the Chairman. However, the standing order relating to closure of debate and the orders relating to the suspension of a member can be put in force only when the Chairman is in the Chair.

The Constitution confers the following powers and functions on the Chairman of the Dáil:

1. membership of the Commission which exercises the powers and performs the functions of the President in his absence or incapacity (Article 14.2.1°);

2. ex officio membership of the Council of State which aids and counsels the President in the exercise and performance of certain of his powers and functions (Article 31.2);

3. certification of bills which, in his opinion, are money bills (Article 22.2);

4. possession and exercise of a casting vote in the event of an equality of votes in the Dáil (Article 15.11.2°).

The office of the Chairman of the Dáil, as prescribed in the standing orders and under the Constitution, is characterised by its authority and impartiality. He represents the House in all its external relations. He takes no part in political activity or in debate. His rulings are respected by all sides of the House, may not be criticised by any member except on a formal motion, and are regarded as precedents to be followed by subsequent Chairmen.

Chairman of Seanad (Cathaoirleach)

The standing orders of the Seanad devolve duties and confer authority upon the Chairman in matters concerning the

conduct of proceedings and the general business and administration of the House. These duties and powers do not differ
significantly from those conferred on the Chairman of the
Dáil.

The Constitution confers the following powers and functions on the Chairman of the Seanad:

1. membership of the Commission which exercises the powers
and performs the functions of the President in his absence or
incapacity (Article 14.2.1°);

2. ex officio membership of the Council of State which aids
and counsels the President in the exercise and performance of
certain of his powers and functions (Article 31.2);

3. possession and exercise of a casting vote in the event of an
equality of votes in the Seanad (Article 15.11.2°).

Debates and Journals

Debates

An official report of the debates of each House in oratio
recta is published under the supervision of the Chairman.
Daily unrevised reports are published initially within two or
three days of the sittings to which they refer. They are periodi-
cally revised, collated, indexed, bound and published in vol-
umes. A debate is referred to by giving the number of the
volume and the relevant columns.

Journals

Journals of proceedings of the Houses contain daily records
of the res gestae of the Houses compiled from the minutes
made by the Clerks. They constitute the permanent official
record and are accepted in all courts as prima facie evidence
of what has been done in the Houses (section 2 of the Docu-
mentary Evidence Act, 1925). A copy of each journal (or
imeachta) is initialled and signed by the Chairman of the
House. In common with all the other records and documents
belonging to the Houses, the journals are retained in the custody of the Clerks and may not be removed without the
express permission of the House concerned (or by the Chairman of the House, if the House is adjourned for any period
longer than a week). The journals are published daily and are
subsequently indexed and published annually in bound form.

13 Administration

Dáil Éireann and Seanad Éireann are assisted by a secretariat which is referred to as the Office of the Houses of the Oireachtas. The standing orders of the Dáil provide for the offices of Clerk and Clerk-Assistant of the Dáil, and the standing orders of the Seanad provide for the offices of Clerk and Clerk-Assistant of the Seanad.

The Clerk of the Dáil (and in his absence the Clerk-Assistant) has direction and control over the officers of the Dáil and the joint staff, subject to such orders as he may receive from the Chairman of the Dáil. The Clerk of the Seanad (and in his absence the Clerk-Assistant) has direction and control over the officers of the Seanad and the joint staff subject to such orders as he may receive from the Chairman of the Seanad.

The appointment of the Clerk and Clerk-Assistant of the Dáil is made by the Taoiseach on the joint recommendation of the Chairman of the Dáil and the Minister for the Public Service, and the appointment of the Clerk and Clerk-Assistant of the Seanad is made by the Taoiseach on the joint recommendation of the Chairman of the Seanad and the Minister for the Public Service (sections 5 and 6 of the Staff of the Houses of the Oireachtas Act, 1959).

The functions of the Office of the Houses of the Oireachtas include the preparation of the Order Paper and the Journal of Proceedings of each House, the issue of an Official Report of the Debates of each House, the custody of all records and other documents belonging to the Houses, and administrative, clerical and subordinate work associated with the sittings and business of the Houses and of their committees.

Appendix

Register of Nominating Bodies

Register of Nominating Bodies entitled to nominate persons to the panels of candidates for the purpose of every Seanad general election, revised at the annual revision and signed by the Seanad Returning Officer in pursuance of section 19 of the Seanad Electoral (Panel Members) Act 1947, as amended by the Seanad Electoral (Panel Members) Act 1954 (as revised on 7 July 1978).

Cultural and Educational Panel

Royal Irish Academy	19 Dawson Street, Dublin 2
Cumann Leabharlann na hÉireann (The Library Association of Ireland)	Thomas Prior House, Merrion Road, Dublin 4
Irish National Teachers' Organisation	35 Parnell Square, Dublin 1
Association of Secondary Teachers, Ireland	13 Highfield Road, Rathgar, Dublin 6
An Cumann Ghairm-Oideachais i n-Éireann (The Irish Vocational Education Association)	30, The Mall, Waterford
The Incorporated Law Society of Ireland	Solicitors' Buildings, Four Courts, Dublin 7
Cumann Dochtúirí na hÉireann (The Irish Medical Association)	10 Fitzwilliam Place, Dublin 2
Royal College of Surgeons in Ireland	123 St Stephen's Green, Dublin 2
Dental Board	57 Merrion Square, Dublin 2

Veterinary Council	53 Lansdowne Road, Ballsbridge, Dublin 4
The Pharmaceutical Society of Ireland	18 Shrewsbury Road, Ballsbridge, Dublin 4
The General Council of the Bar of Ireland	Law Library, Four Courts, Dublin 7
Bantracht na Tuaithe (Irish Countrywomen's Association)	58 Merrion Road, Ballsbridge, Dublin 4
Royal Society of Antiquaries of Ireland	63 Merrion Square, Dublin 2
Muintir na Gaeltachta	51 Sráid Móintseó, Baile Átha Cliath 7
The Royal Irish Academy of Music	36/38 Westland Row, Dublin 2
Irish Dental Association	29 Kenilworth Square, Dublin 6
The Irish Georgian Society	Castletown House, Celbridge, Co. Kildare
Cumann le Seandacht Átha Cliath (The Old Dublin Society)	City Assembly House, 58 Sth. William Street, Dublin 2
Irish Federation of University Teachers	195 Pearse Street, Dublin 2

Agricultural Panel

Royal Dublin Society	Post Office Box No. 121, Ballsbridge, Dublin 4
The Irish Agricultural Organisation Society Limited	The Plunkett House, 84 Merrion Square, Dublin 2
National Executive of the Irish Live Stock Trade	627 North Circular Road, Dublin 1
The Irish Bloodstock Breeders' Association	Kildare Paddocks, Kill, Co. Kildare
The Sugar Beet and Vegetable Section Limited, Irish Farmers' Association	The Irish Farm Centre, Naas Road, Bluebell, Dublin 12

The Irish Creamery Managers' Association	33 Kildare Street, Dublin 2
Munster Agricultural Society	21 Cook Street, Cork
The Council of Boards of Fishery Conservators	81 Highfield Park, Dundrum, Dublin 14
General Council of Committees of Agriculture	'Sheena', Charleville Road, Tullamore, Co. Offaly

Labour Panel

Irish Congress of Trade Unions	Congress House, 19 Raglan Road, Dublin 4
The Irish Conference of Professional and Service Associations	93 St Stephen's Green, Dublin 2

Industrial and Commercial Panel

Association of Chambers of Commerce of Ireland	7 Clare Street, Dublin 2
The Confederation of Irish Industry	Confederation House, Kildare Street, Dublin 2
The Construction Industry Federation	9 Leeson Park, Dublin 6.
The Society of the Irish Motor Industry	5 Upper Pembroke Street, Dublin 2
RGDATA—Retail, Grocery, Dairy and Allied Trades Association	RGDATA House, 24 Earlsfort Terrace, Dublin 2
The Irish Auctioneers and Valuers Institute	38 Merrion Square, East, Dublin 2
Irish Banks' Standing Committee	Nassau House, Nassau Street, Dublin 2
The Insurance Institute of Ireland	32 Nassau Street, Dublin 2
The Institute of Chartered Accountants in Ireland	7 Fitzwilliam Place, Dublin 2
The Royal Institute of the Architects of Ireland	8 Merrion Square, Dublin 2
The Federated Union of Employers	8 Fitzwilliam Place, Dublin 2

The Irish Hotels Federation	13 Northbrook Road, Dublin 6
The Association of Advertisers in Ireland Limited	44 Lower Leeson Street, Dublin 2
The Institute of Advertising Practitioners in Ireland	35 Upper Fitzwilliam Street, Dublin 2
National Development Association (Forbairt)	Ireland House Trade Centre, Strand Road, Sandymount, Dublin 4
The National Wholesale Confectioners' Association	28 Harcourt Street, Dublin 2
The Institution of Engineers of Ireland	22 Clyde Road, Ballsbridge, Dublin 4
The Institute of Certified Public Accountants in Ireland	22 Upper Fitzwilliam Street, Dublin 2
The Institute of Professional Auctioneers, Valuers and Livestock Salesmen	44 Lower Leeson Street, Dublin 2
The Wholesale Fruit, Potato and Produce Merchants' Association of Ireland Ltd.	11A Lower Fitzwilliam Street, Dublin 2
Vintners' Federation of Ireland	L.V.A. Centre, Anglesea Road, Ballsbridge, Dublin 4
The Irish Restaurant Owners Association	11 Herbert Street, Dublin 2
Irish Road Haulage Association	58 Burrin Street, Carlow.
The National Tourism Council of Ireland (Comhairle Náisiúnta Cuairtíochta na hÉireann)	Confederation House, Kildare Street, Dublin 2
Marketing Institute of Ireland Limited	Confederation House, Kildare Street, Dublin 2
Cumann na nGníomhairí Paitinne Cláruighthe (Association of Registered Patent Agents)	27 Clyde Road, Ballsbridge, Dublin 4
The Irish Architect's Society Limited	35 Fitzwilliam Place, Dublin 2

The Irish Hotel and Catering
Institute

11 Herbert Street, Dublin 2

The Electrical Industries
Federation of Ireland

'McKinley House', 16 Main
Street, Blackrock, Co.
Dublin

Administrative Panel

Irish County Councils
General Council

2/3 Parnell Square, Dublin 1

Association of Municipal
Authorities of Ireland

Town Hall, Mallow, Co. Cork

Central Remedial Clinic

Vernon Avenue, Clontarf,
Dublin 3

The National Association
for Cerebral Palsy (Ireland)
Limited

Sandymount School and
Clinic, Sandymount
Avenue, Dublin 4

The Multiple Sclerosis
Society of Ireland

14 Merrion Square, Dublin 2

Irish Wheelchair Association

Áras Chúchulainn, Blackheath
Drive, Clontarf, Dublin 3

The National Association for
the Mentally Handicapped
of Ireland

5 Fitzwilliam Place, Dublin 2

National Association for the
Deaf

25 Lower Leeson Street,
Dublin 2